BEHIND THE PAINT

THE FIRST CHAPTER- ITALY 2011

THE SKETCHBOOK & JOURNAL OF ARTIST

MICHAEL TIEMAN

Published in the United States.

Published by Michael Tieman Publishing
www.artistsgallerie.com

Editor: Patty Coomes

ISBN-13: 978-0615891316
ISBN-10: 0615891314

First printing Oct. 2013
Printed in the United States

First Edition

CONTENTS

The role of an artist from the dawn of time has been as a visual story-teller. The artist starts the story, writing the first chapter and the viewer finishes it by adding to it their imagination and life experiences.

This is the first chapter of our travel to Rome and the hills of Tuscany, Italy. Here are my sketches, stories and thoughts that I work with to create my paintings.

Feel free to read, imagine and find out what is ...

"Behind The Paint"

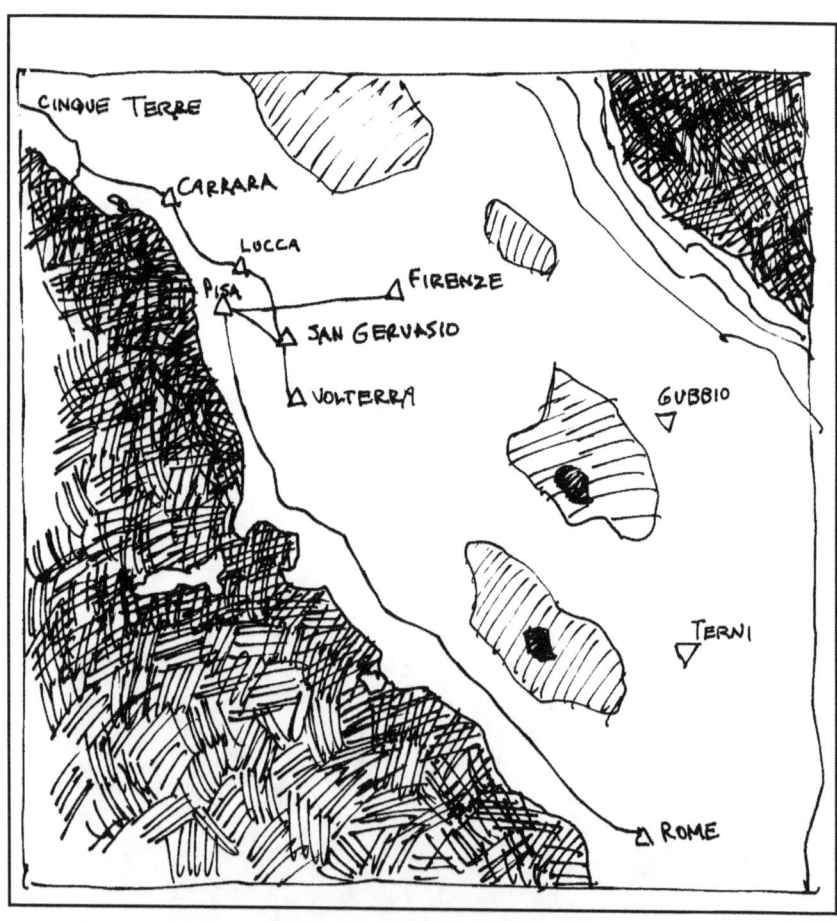

HOW WE TRAVEL

Nancy and I have had the pleasure of being able to live and travel outside the country during our almost 40 years together.

We have lived in the U.S. and Canada, traveled in mainland China, Hong Kong, England, France and now Italy.

Our travel philosophy is go and enjoy the area, eat the local food (even street food which was interesting in Hong Kong), drink the local wines, hang out in the local joints, and enjoy the locals. We smile a lot and say please and thank you in the native language and seem to have done OK. People are the same world wide - a smile gets you a smile.

We sit down before we go to a new country and research the areas of our interests - art, history and of course shopping. Our daily travel schedule expectations have changed as we have gotten older and our energy levels changed. Nancy and I decide which art and historical monuments we MUST see, and what would be good to see. Then we try to plan our schedules so we hit one major museum or monument per day, giving us plenty of time to do other things of interest. Instead of taking 90 minutes to see a museum we may spend over 3 hours looking at select pieces or artists. We focus on the quality of time in a place, not how many places can we see. We can never see all we want in one visit, but we can enjoy what we see. And of course there is shopping, especially the little town markets with their stalls of local foods and hand made goods.

For the last 11 years we have wanted to eat and drink our way through Tuscany with a sketchbook and camera. My father died this year and because he loved to travel, we put everything else aside and took this trip in his memory. I am sure he was smiling down on us in approval and laughing at times during some of our wacky adventures.

We rented a car in Italy, a little Fiat Panda, and drove through the country side. Those experiences you will read about and they will make you laugh and sometimes shake your head. All in all, we will go back.

PORTLAND - ROME

Day 1 - Sept. 15, 2011

We arrived in Rome, Italy today at 7:30 am. Left Portland, Oregon at 7:30 am yesterday. Very long flight and crammed into seats like sardines. At the Rome airport after going through customs they glanced at our passports and waved us through - no stamps on our passports, how disappointing. We have to take the train from the airport to the central train station in Rome as our hotel is a couple of blocks from there. The train tickets were advertised at €9.50 each, but actual cost turned out to be €14 each. Not to be the only time advertised prices mean only a suggestion and are not real. No truth in advertising. We remembered from a show we saw last year, Globe Trekker that we are to have the tickets we just bought stamped in the little yellow machines; otherwise you will be fined from €5 to €100 by the train conductor. Thanks Public Broadcasting Station.

Dirty, smelly train station, corridors not well marked as to where things are, or how to get where you need to go. Nancy and I hopped a train leaving the station and hoped it was going to Rome ... we were lucky. A 30 min. ride through the slum area of Rome – gang graffiti on most walls and on the passing trains. I take Nancy to only the best places. Seems we did this same thing in Paris and Hong Kong. Hey we are consistent if nothing.

At the train station we got our Roma Pass – great cards – €25 includes 2 museum or landmark fees, all metro transportation, and % off other museum fees. A 3 day pass also gets you past the long lines of people waiting for tickets. Rome does not have a museum pass as do London and Paris, which gives you unlimited entry into most museums for 3 days for one price, but this one is OK. Wonder if the major US cities have one?

We took the Metro to our hotel, exit station was 2 blocks from our hotel but we went out of the station on the wrong side, did I say that Italy signage sucks? We ended up touring a bit of the back streets before we

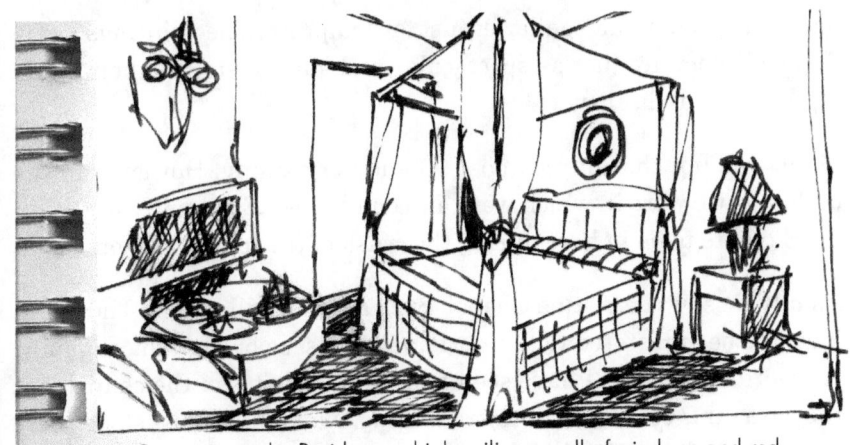

Our room at the Residenza - high ceilings, wall of windows and red flocked wallpaper.

ended at the hotel. "Residenza Vaticana" is nice funky hotel, entrance on the second floor of an old building (had to ask directions when we got into the building). Really nice people at the hotel. We were early to check in and our room wasn't ready, so the maid had us sit down, offered us some water and breakfast if we wanted and she cleaned our room next. The room was small, but clean, comfortable, quiet and centrally located in Rome. We arrived at the hotel 3 hrs. after landing, showered, changed and headed out to the Vatican – we had tickets for 2pm (bought online on the Vatican web site before we left the U.S. so we did not wait in lines … very easy).

The Vatican was a 10 min. walk, so we had lunch at a sidewalk cafe. Our first meal in Italy … what else? We had a Margherite pizza with house wine, and sat at a sidewalk cafe watching all the crazy people around us. There were a ton of small mini cars and scooters moving like crazy and the drivers were insane. You cross the street at your own peril – very few stop lights – we crossed the streets with the nuns and locals pushing baby strollers crossing. We may be slow, but not stupid.

Then the Vatican Museum. Art overload – so much to see in every nook and room – look up and on the floor and all around. I saw one of my favorite sculpture pieces – "Laocoon and His Sons" – so impressive close up, and we could get close. Room after room, the animal room, chariot room, Egyptian room - galleries just for sculpture. The paintings in the Raphael room are just as spectacular and since restored, their colors are brilliant and sensuous.

Rome was hot that day, almost 90 and very sunny. Hot even in the buildings we were in which were air conditioned. Everyone was sweating, I'd hate to be in here during the crush of the tourist season.

Finally we saw the Sistine Chapel. Such a very small chapel. The paintings had been restored to their original colors- so bright almost gaudy. We were awestruck. I have seen many great photos of the chapel, but they are tame compared to the real thing. Nancy and I just stood there and took it all in. The things that impressed me were the huge figures in the very small chapel, the intense colors and the power of the figures and faces. We got lost in the paintings.

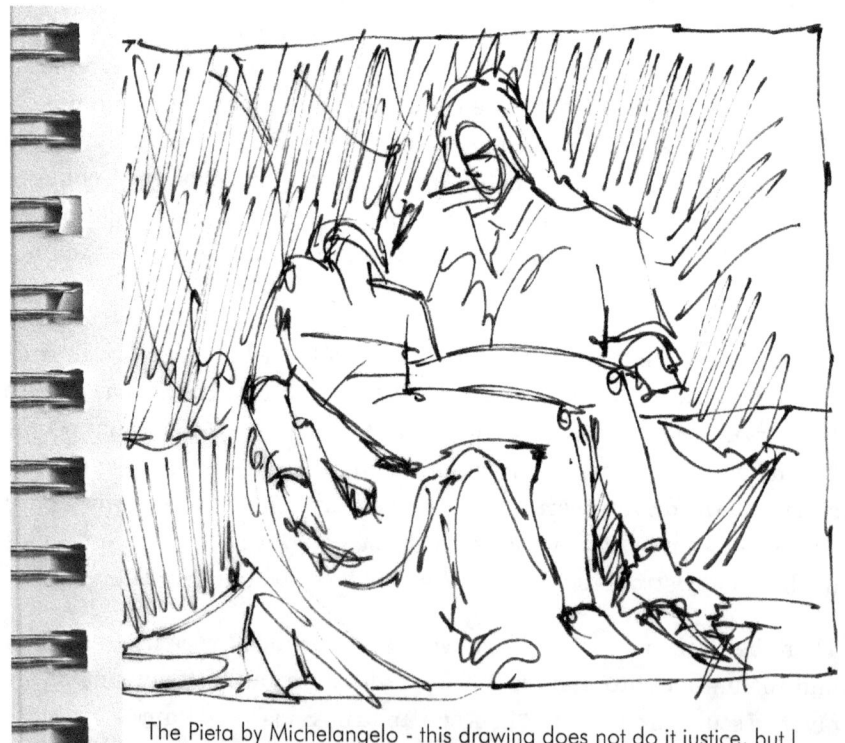

The Pieta by Michelangelo - this drawing does not do it justice, but I tried to show the passion of the moment.

There are signs all over the area that you are not allowed to take photos and being in a chapel, we were to be quiet. The guards spent most of their time telling people to be quiet and quit taking photos. So sad, some people just don't think the rules apply to them, happens everywhere.

Left the Vatican Museum and went to the Basilica to see the Pieta by Michelangelo. Another unbelievable piece, unfortunately it is behind glass, but you can still see the softness and coolness of the marble. You need to see it in person to get the whole spirit of the piece. Hoards of people and tours from all over the world. We heard Chinese, German, Italian, Russian and Australian.

Nancy bought me a white fedora from one of the many street vendors, the heat and intense sun made my face red and I needed something to keep me cool.

We walked back to the hotel – and crashed for awhile – walking a lot on cobblestones is hard on the feet and the hips. The fashions on the street were unreal. Ladies dressed to the nines in tall spiked heels for work in the retail shops. Walking on those stones – crazy what you will do in the name of fashion. Most of the stores close from 1-3:30 pm. Went to dinner early – 6pm – because we were bushed. The hotel suggested a nice little place around the corner, Via Marco Polo, great mussels in a marinara sauce.

So, in Rome today we ate pizza, mussels, artichokes and risotto. Drank wonderful house wines, thus began our eating and drinking our way through Tuscany. Tomorrow we do the Caesar shuffle starting with the Metro to the Coliseum. I took 250 photos and some great sketches of the surrounding buildings with their red tile roofs and exquisite trees.

Day 2 - Sept. 16

Today we did the Coliseum, Forum area, Spanish Steps and the Trevi Fountain. Started today out not on the right foot as we found that our converter had died. But our wonderful maid (excuse me here, but I am really bad with names, so I apologize now to all we met), came to the

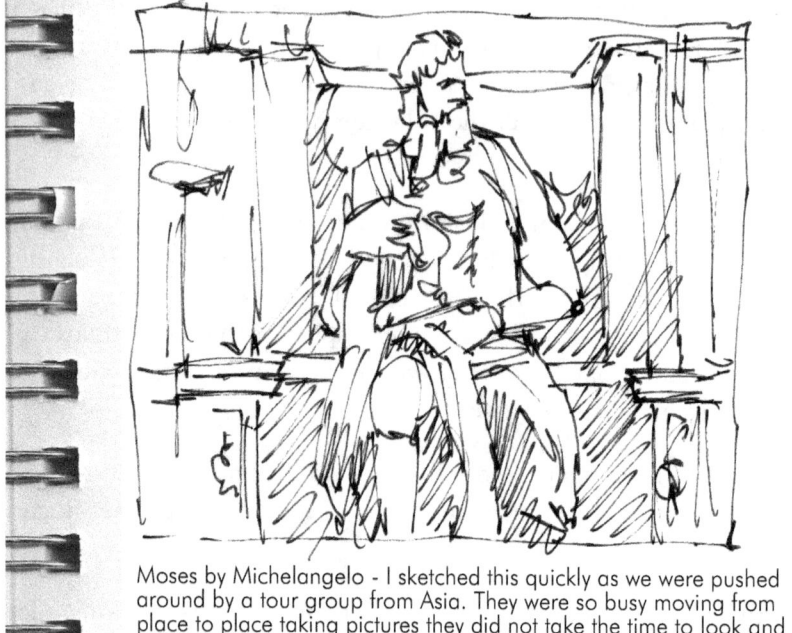

Moses by Michelangelo - I sketched this quickly as we were pushed around by a tour group from Asia. They were so busy moving from place to place taking pictures they did not take the time to look and enjoy the art.

rescue as she had one left behind by another guest who did not want it back. We were just going to borrow it and buy another one, but the maid and owner insisted we keep it. These two people were so helpful and good to us the whole time, they made the stay here very enjoyable.

Continental breakfast of fresh juices, cheese and ham, croissants, cereal, coffee and bread. They also have a really cool machine that at a push of a button will make you espresso, cappuccino or cafe american.

Off we went on the "A" train Metro to the other side of Rome. We wanted to start at the church San Pietro in Vincoli that houses the "Moses" by Michelangelo (you will notice a theme here when it comes to art). We got off at the Coliseum exit and yes, we promptly got turned around and started in the wrong direction ... signage? Nancy spotted our error soon enough and we only went a block out of our way. Have I said their signage sucks and their maps are not much better.

After a few turns we saw a little sign pointing the way, but the signs stopped at a 3-way intersection - were we surprised? This time we guessed correctly and we went down the street where a large group of people were coming out of. The next dilemma, two unmarked churches - which one was the one we wanted? We chose the first one - you guessed it we chose wrong - a helpful local sent us in the right direction. Again a smile wins the day. I suggest if you ever go with us on a trip always take the opposite direction we do, you might get there sooner, but we always seem to find our way.

The outside of this church appeared tiny, but when we went inside it opened up into this big open area - the affect worked. It takes your breath away. The church was filled with many spectacular paintings and sculptures with frescos and tiled paintings on the ceiling and floor. You had to go through the entire church up to the alter of gold and there off in an alcove on the right sat "Moses". In was in the dark, but I took some pictures anyhow (it is allowed here), then the person next to me dropped a 50 cent piece into a little machine and the whole area was lit up in a spectacular light display. Their lighting was awesome, caressing the curves of the marble and almost making it come to life. A gazillion camera flashes went off to destroy the mood, but there was enough flashless moments to make it all worthwhile. I spent quite a bit of time just standing there and soaking it all in. I take photos as a record, but then I put the camera down and just sit or stand and take in the piece trying to see it as the artist created it.

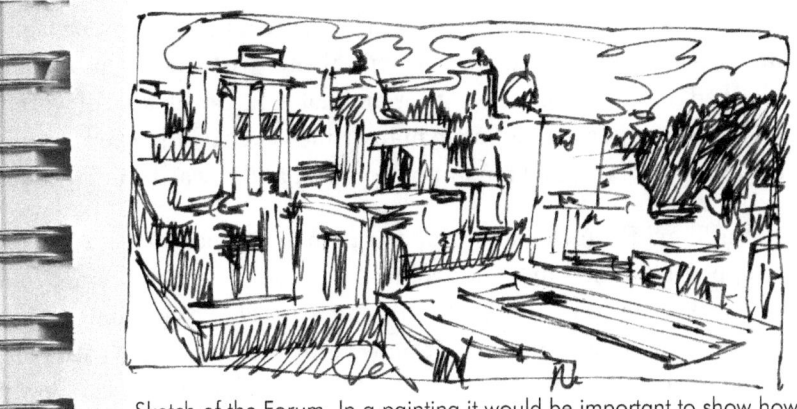

Sketch of the Forum. In a painting it would be important to show how the new modern Rome buildings are built on the past structures. Nothing has changed here in milleniums as you can see even these old structures are built on still older ones.

A technical note here: The camera I took with me is a Nikon D80 digital and I only took one lens, a 18-135 telephoto. I had two chips, a 2GB and a 16GB chip which together I could get 18,000 photos. The entire trip I rarely used the flash and except when I was bumped, the shots were very clean, sharp and even . Nancy had her little digital camera and I also used the camera on my Droid when I did not schlep my camera. I can still remember all the rolls of film I use to take with me on trips, crossing my fingers as the film went through security hoping they would not fog it even though I used lead pouches, and then the expense of developing and printing. It is now much easier and less stressful.

We left the church and worked our way back to the Coliseum. With our Roma Pass in hand, we walked past the long line of people waiting to get in (we found out it was a 3 hour wait), and walked right in.

I am not a writer so it is hard to describe in words what I felt as we walked around the building that remains the center of so much of the history and cruelty of the world. Even with the crowds it was a humbling experience. Spent several hours wandering through the passageways and up and down the steps. Sat on several of the discarded blocks to rest, how many have sat on those same pieces over the centuries and what were their stories? This was history close up and personal.

Then we went outside, bought some gelato at a little stand (the lemon was great, pistachio ok) and headed for the Forum. Wasn't there a movie titled "On the Way to the Forum"? Again our passes got us right through the lines and into the archeological site. We walked and walked and walked in the 90 degree weather and hot sun. Drank a lot of water, which we resupplied in our bottle many times at convenient water stations for free. We reached a point of overload and it was time to leave.

Off to the Trevi Fountain, following our map and typical street signage. We stopped for lunch in a little place in a back alley had wine, cold water, spaghetti carbonara and fried calamari. Very good spaghetti, but the calamari had too much batter, however it was not chewy so all was fine, and it gave us a chance to get out of the heat and sun and sit down. Also did not have to pay €1 for the bathroom.

The Trevi fountain was a spectacular site even with the crowds. I do not like crowds so Nancy quickly got up to the front of the masses and threw in a coin so she will come back, picture op, and then she took a photo of me as I did the same. As I was throwing my coin, I got hit with a €2 coin on the cheek which someone threw from the back of the crowd. It was not cool and they were a really bad shot to miss a big fountain like that. As I looked closely at the sculptures, it looked like they were carved out of 3 cubic square blocks of marble then joined together. The craftsmanship.

Our last foray of the day is to the Spanish steps nearby ... according to the map anyhow. We got close, in a square but no steps. Then we saw a crowd of people around the corner from the square and viola. I was blown away by how small the steps were, in all the photos they look huge, but in reality not so much. Nancy and I climbed halfway up and sat down on the steps and yes we kissed. Hey, we are in Italy, got to get with the program. About 4pm now, we started around 10ish, and it was time to call it quits. On to the Metro, a station nearby, to the hotel and crashed until 7.

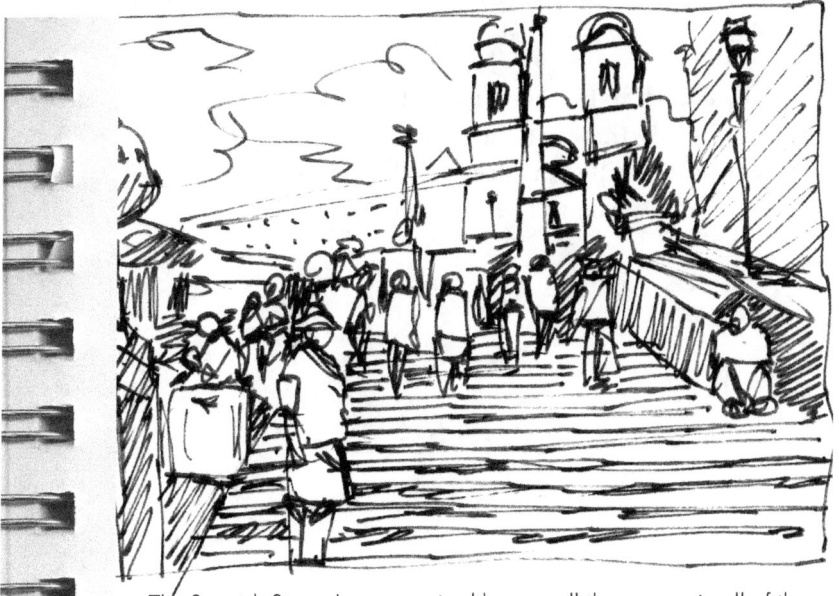

The Spanish Steps. I was surprised how small they were - in all of the photos I've seen they look huge.

Using the hotel free Wi-Fi, Google maps showed a restaurant nearby that had raves about their veal, Al Palazzaccio. We had asked the hotel the previous night about places to eat and they turned us on to a nice little place a couple of blocks away, so I thought I would see if modern technology worked tonight.

On the way to dinner, we walked the streets and stopped at the little stalls and Nancy picked up some things then off to dinner. At this time of night, the locals come out to walk and shop and eat dinner. Most restaurants don't get busy before 8pm. So we went local.

If I was a food writer, I would write pages about this place. It was small, six tables inside and six outside, (we ate inside tonight). They had an extensive menu, but one of the specials was the veal meal - fixed price. The first course was gnocchi for Nancy and ravioli for me ... the gnocchi melted in our mouths ... butter and cheese and cheese. Then the veal. Veal in butter and cheese and thyme with fried prosciutto on top. You could cut the veal with a fork. Add the roasted potatoes, canolli for desert with espresso or cappuccino and house wine. The best dinner we have had in many years anywhere. And the waiter, a little old man with a twinkle in his eyes melted Nancy's heart.

We walked back to the hotel along the busy streets and put our tired bodies to bed. Both of us had blisters on our feet. The roads/walks on old cobblestones killed our feet and hips and my knee - but sleep will refresh. Tomorrow on to Pisa by train from Rome.

ROME-SAN GERVASIO

Day 3 - Sept. 17

How do I start our travels today? Stated out with a nice sleep, continential breakfast and a walk around the hotel to find Nancy some sandals. We got her some, and got back to the hotel in plenty of time to get on the Metro and to the train station an hour before we departed.

The quest begins - with train tickets in hand (we bought them in the U.S. from AAA), and schlepping suitcases, we get off the Metro and follow the signage and walk. We find the departure signs and it says platform 24, just in case, I ask an info man in front of platform 24, he says it could be 24 or 27 - depends - so I leave and hand Nancy the tickets and she asks the same man - check the departure board for the train number. We did #25 not #24 - we asked three uniformed men - one even showed us the departure board - #25, just to make sure, we asked a cop - check the departure board. There were no trains at any of the aforementioned platforms. Needless to say, we missed our train. Rome train terminal signage sucks - remember that, I will come back to it. We followed information signs - to empty corridors - no one to ask, no information booths, a strange country when you have no Italian language skills. A smile was not the answer here.

Panic sets in - we ask more people and follow more information signs then we happen to end up at the very end of the terminal and here are moving reader boards. Where were signs we ask? Seems the Metro trains dump you on the rail tracks at the opposite end of a large terminal. A helpful young man in an info uniform finds us and showed us the information booth - a solo man in a kiosk the size of his chair and a little unlit sign above him - 2' x 5'. He told us in broken English we needed to get into the lines behind him and get a new ticket. The next train leaves in less than an hour. By the way, the train we need to Pisa is the Genova train. After many English expletives to no one inparticular, we get into this long winding line of frustrated travelers. We talked to a young couple behind us in line and it seems they purchased

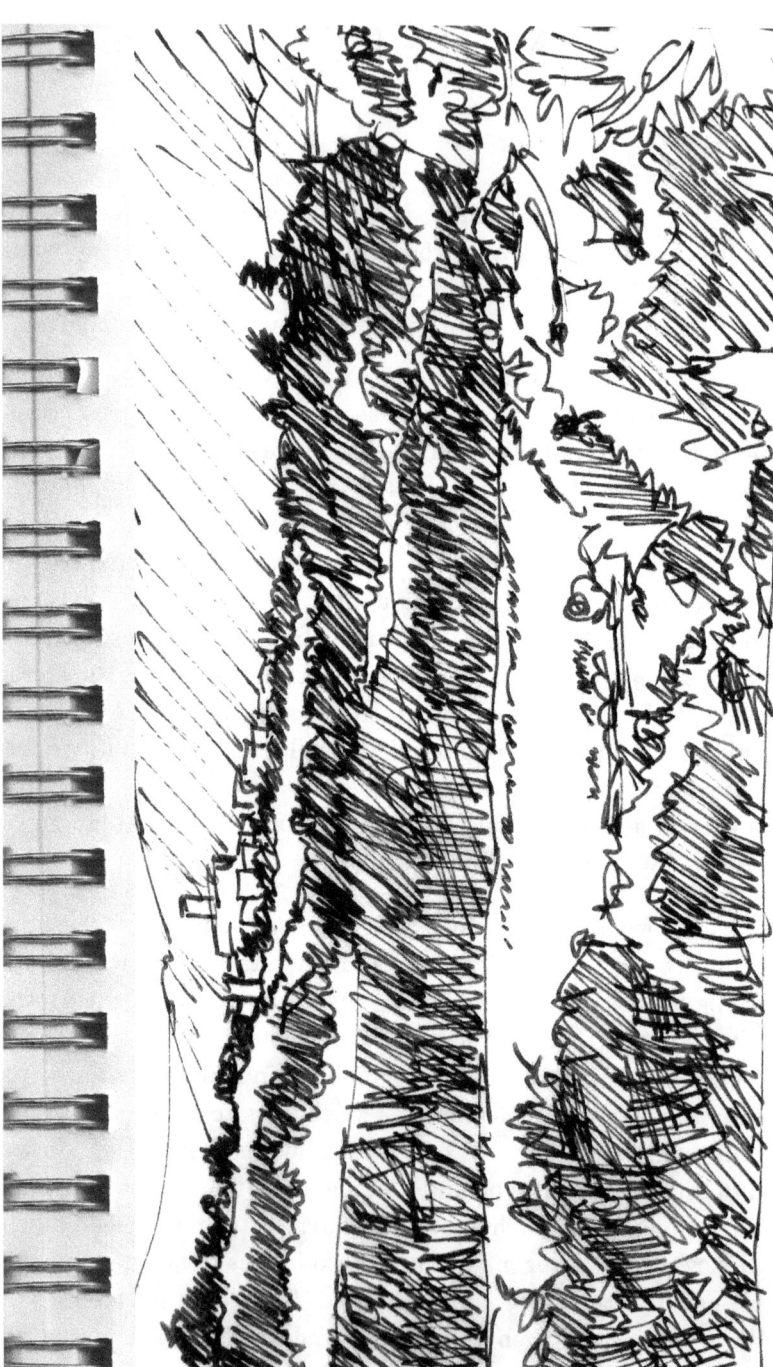

This will be a good painting. The Tuscan hills surround this small hilltop village of Monticristello. I will have to add green hills however as they are brown - the second month of a drought. I am in the San Gervasio area looking across the valley.

tickets online through this train station's website to Siena, but they found at the station that there is no train from Rome to Siena. They had to start all over and lost the money they had paid. They had the same thing to say about Rome trains we did.

When we finally got to the head of the line, and spoke to the gentleman - he just wrote on our tickets the new time. We missed the 1:00 now it was the 2:00 train, 2 hours late. The platform number? You look at the board 20 min before the train leaves for the track number. And we pay an extra €8 or €16 when we board the train. We had 45 min. so we ate lunch - shared a sandwich and 3 bottles of water. But we had a plan and tickets with reserved seat numbers.

The time came, we were in front of the reader board and looking for the train to Genova, no train #, just a train to Genova leaves at 2:10 on platform #23. Off we go, hell bent for leather. Into our lives drops this helpful young man who found our car #, opened the locked rail car with a code, helped us and others on to the train found all of us our seats looked at our tickets and asked us for the €8 it said on our tickets. Nancy gave him money, a larger bill than €8 - wait for it now - we never saw him again - he did not work for the train (how did he have the code to unlock the train car?). We got scammed. Why are these people allowed to operate so blatantly? We have traveled in China, Hong Kong, London and Paris and throughout Canada and the U.S. and have never run into this attitude before. Fortunately, when the conductor came by to check our tickets she does not collect the €8 or €16. So it all works out I guess. But, the train stinks of old sweat, the air conditioner is broken (only 90 degrees outside), the door to the toilets don't lock nor do the toilets flush. Remember what I said earlier about Rome trains?

We are in the Pisa train station and need to get to the airport to pick up our rental car. The Pisa station was small, with well marked signage and we went right to the main terminal, bought our tickets for the shuttle train (€1.20 ea.). Walked to the well marked track platform, sat for about 20 min. and got on and off at the airport. Don't worry, the Pisa airport signage also sucks, we walked almost through the terminal before we saw a little sign to the rental cars. At the rental building there is a long line of people at the Hertz counter and the other rental car counters are empty of customers. Someone knows how to do business in Italy.

We get our Fiat "Panda" about the size of one of my shoes - but we fit as does our luggage. We go around in circles finding the exit. Now we have directions to our B&B, Podere la Pergola in San Gervasio written out by the owner Caroline - seems clear and simple. Take this exit not this one, go around the round about and take this road, slow down and take the left - all we did except we took the wrong left - so we traveled some of the more interesting back roads of Tuscany - even went through this nice little town twice - once each way - found a lady coming out of her home in Montecristello - I asked her directions in English - she rattled off something in Italian and went back into her home, but left the front door open ... so I followed and she came back out ... seems she forgot her reading glasses. She looked at our directions, said San Gervasio and pointed to the left road, rattled off something and made a T with her hands and gestured left.

Off Nancy and I went the way we came from after thanking the lady in the glasses. Dirt road, twisty turning one car wide and viola we come to a T junction. My mama did not raise a complete dummy, we took a

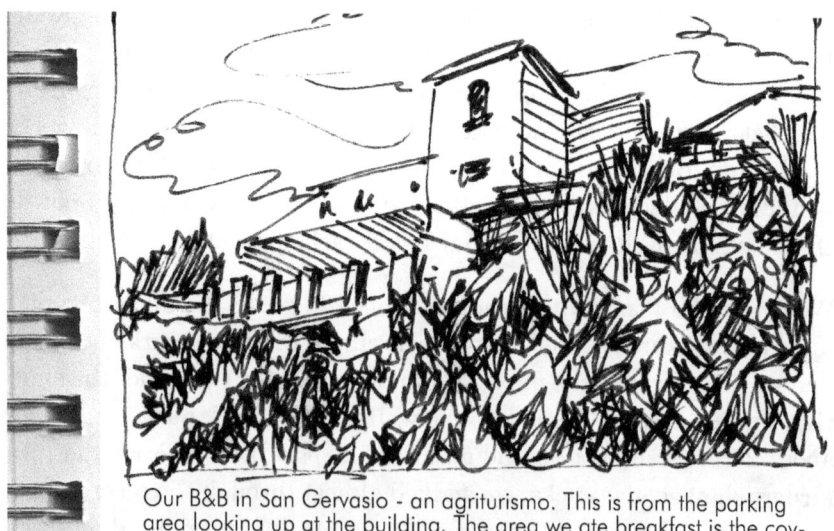

Our B&B in San Gervasio - an agriturismo. This is from the parking area looking up at the building. The area we ate breakfast is the covered porch on the left. The house is done in a Spanish style with red tile roofs and beautiful arched windows and doorways.

left. There was a sign saying San Gervasio. We were almost there! An elderly couple were walking their dog on the road so we stopped and Nancy asked the lady for directions to the B&B showing her the directions. The lady did a jester we now understood and Nancy gave the lady her glasses low and behold, we were 50 feet from the entrance to the B&B. The owner was worried about us because it was getting dark. She had texted me several times since we hit Pisa to see how we were doing. Caroline is a wonderful lady, speaks 5 languages, and has a warm heart. As she was leading us to our room, Nancy and I turned around and saw the most breathtaking sunset.

I am almost done so please keep on reading.

We ate dinner at this little restaurant up the hill from the B&B. No cars except one and Nancy asked if they were open .. sure, no problem. We were the only ones in the restaurant save the waiter, cook (mama) and papa. Our fare this night was what they had, a plate of fantastic

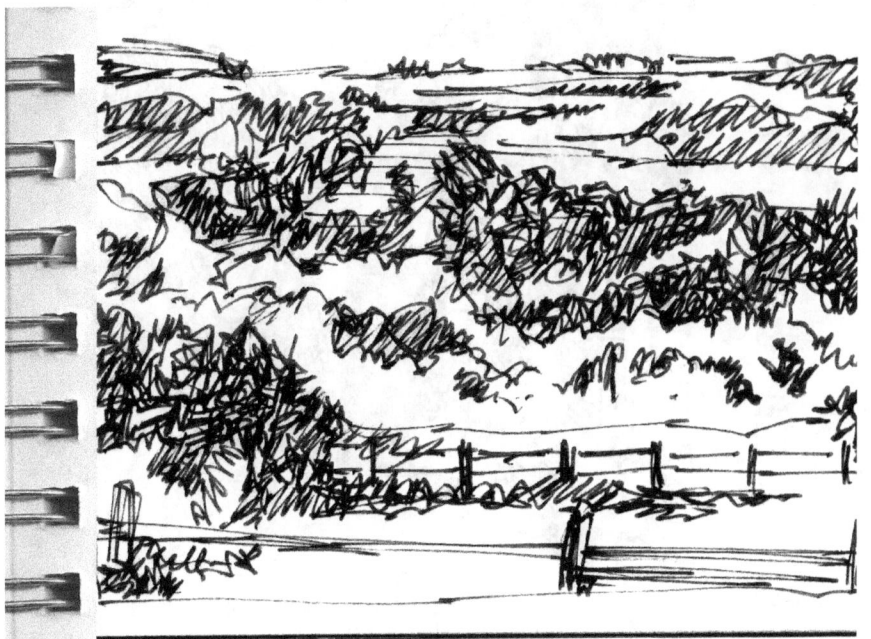

This is our view at breakfast of the Tuscan countryside from the porch.

antipasto - cheeses, prosciutto, 3 types of salumi, bacon, pickled onion, olives ... all local products and a local wine. The only thing in the kitchen - pasta with ham cheese and butter sauce. It was fantastic - the chef "Mama" was cooking rabbit for the dinner next day for the locals hunters - rabbit hunting season starts tomorrow. So, the waiter, the son was the cook. Oh, and when we told him about our Rome travels - when we said we took the train from Rome to Pisa - he rolled his eyes and said some not good words about the train and Rome terminal.

Remember what I said about Rome trains, even the Italians say ditto to that.

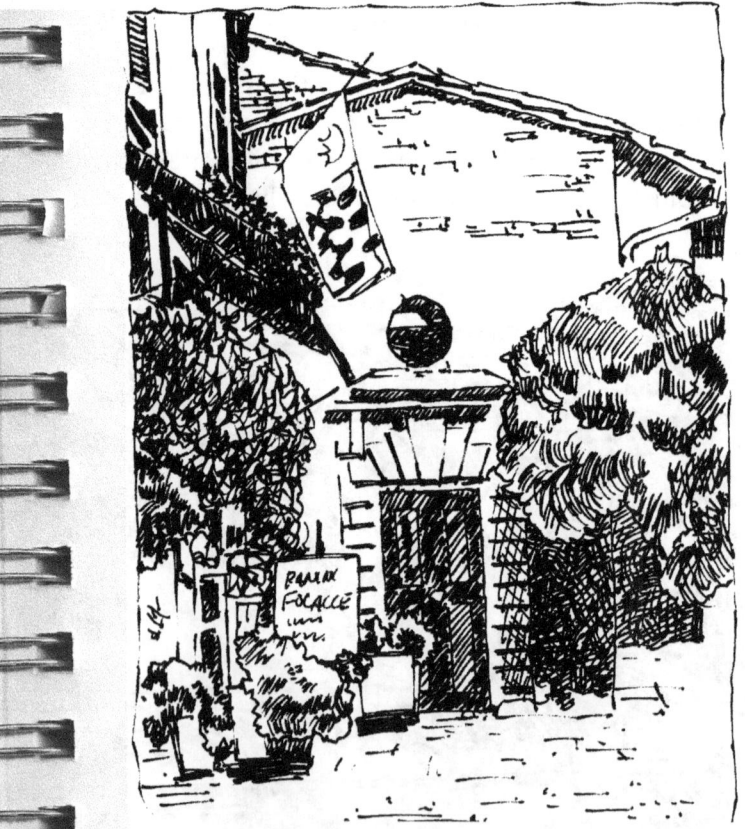

Funky old restaurant at the end of a small street in Volterra. This will be a painting because I like the colors of the flags and the flowers in the terra cotta pots. Against the stark stone walls and the beautiful old wooden doors. If these old doors could talk, think of the people and events they witnessed.

SAN GERVASIO-VOLTERRA

Day 4 - Sept. 18

Breakfast at 9:30, healthy - all fruit compote - all from locals - coffee, ham & cheese slices and brochette with fresh tomato & home made (here) olive oil - wonderful - and this is from an egg and bacon man. You can taste the flavors & the tomatoes were rich and juicy and tasted like a tomato should.

Then with road directions from Caroline off we went to Volterra - the walled city known for their alabaster carving artists. The Fiat we rented was perfect for the narrow windy roads. Oh forgot, after breakfast Nancy did some laundry, I sat on the deck and sketched & took photos of the area. The first day of rabbit hunting season and we heard many shots around the hills. After laundry was washed and hung up to dry, we took off. Suppose to rain today - first time in 2 months - the Oregonians come to town and we bring the rain ... they should pay us.

Took quite a few photos on the back roads to Volterra, some great paintings to come. The hills were brown and dried up not the lushness I had thought. Spring here must be gorgeous with all the greens.

Even with the Rick Steves book on Volterra it took us some time to find the parking lots - his book tells us lot #3 is free, but does not show it on his map. But, Nancy found it. Let me tell you, there are a lot of stairs in that walled city, and we only climbed a small number. Took quite a few shots of alleys and these wonderful doors with metal door knockers - and clothes hanging from the windows, and banners. Being Sunday off season, not many people, wandering. We bought some alabaster pieces. The town is known for it's alabaster workshops - the alabaster I have been carving seems a better quality then what I found here and a better color. Bought a good roadmap at the tobacco store, not any good cigars - mostly maps & cigs. - and I bought a lighter so I could smoke a cigar I brought from CB. Half way through town we stopped and had a lunch/snack - cappuccinos and pastries. Wonderful little pastries, fruits

& chocolate, how good is that? On the way out of the shop, thunder rolled through the hills and it started to spit rain. We walked a bit more in and out of the shops, then it started to sound serious so we started back to the car - got sprinkled on then when we hit the car - a downpour. Two months of drought huh? As I write this at 10:30pm, it is still raining - oh well, no cigar tonight.

On our new great map - Nancy found a path back to our B&B - more direct and less of an adventure - or short cuts - our kids know about the short cuts we take ... hmmm.

The drive back was pretty good - only a few cars passed us - and the little car handled real well in the rain. Remembered that the roads would be slippery with the first rain - Nancy kept me over to the right, close to the shoulder as the car was not easy to gauge it's width. Just when I thought I had it figured out, the road narrowed - so my co-pilot kept me close to the edge of the road and out of danger in the center. Only ran into a few crazy drivers that kept on my ass, before they passed - even ran into several slow drivers that were all over the road and we quickly passed them. Must be more of those crazy tourists you hear about.

Back to our B&B, around 6ish, we had a glass of wine before dinner at the neighborhood restaurant at 7:30 , they open at 7. There were four tables of tourists including us, and a huge party of locals filled the rest of the place - some special occasion got the locals dressed up and out to dinner. Much fun. This has been the only place we have been in Italy where the food has been so -so, but it was our fault in what we ordered. Got a mixed meat plate and the meats - chicken, steak, pork and ribs were overcooked and dry. Potatoes and gnocchi were ok. Two hour dinner than back to base, read some, and writing this, then to bed.

Tomorrow is the Carrara marble fields north of Pisa and then the Cinque Terre.

Tuesday our host cooks a traditional Tuscan dinner complete with wine and served in their wine cellar. Looking forward to both days.

SAN GERVASIO-CARRARA-CINQUE TERRE

Day 5 - Sept. 19

We are now half way through our Italy trip. There were lightening storms all last night and rain. Woke up to no electricity - thought the storm had done some damage - walked around the place to find Caroline, but she was not around. I met our next door neighbor - Pietra, she and her husband are from Germany and staying here for awhile. She tried to call on her cell phone, but no answer so we went to the "big house". The owners house is separate from ours for our privacy and theirs. Found Caroline and her husband, Daniele, who came back and fixed the problem - blown fuses.

Good breakfast again, this time there was also fresh mango juice which I had never tried before. Quite tasty. Got the Wi-Fi code so now if I stand in just the right spot, my phone will work. My Droid has a Global chip in it and I added a global data plan from Verizon for the length of the trip, worked great in the major cities, but out here I am relying on the local Wi-Fi.

Now it is off to the Carrara marble fields and the Cinque Terre. With map in the hands of my capable navigator we head off. On the toll road up and around Pisa. Of course, no signs for Pisa but now we are savvy travelers in Italy and know the secret, head for Genova. Great road, like our freeways. Speed limit signs of 110 km, but theses are only a suggestion ... and we found out why later, the toll road you are charged €1 per 10 mins. of time, not how many km you travel. Makes sense why we were traveling at 130km/hr and always seem to have a black BMW or Mercedes riding our butt before they pass us. And turn signals, forget it, no one uses them - they just dart out and cut you off and then say some nice Italian words to you along with some cool arm gestures. Here is a rule we found out about as we drove through Italy that no one tells you ... even if you check your rear view mirror every 3 seconds you will suddenly find a black BMW or Mercedes trying to crawl up your butt before they pass you... where they come from, I have no idea, but there they are. At one point it happened so often I thought they were coming out of our tailpipe.

Nice drive to Carrara, some signage challenges, hate the round abouts - four to six roads coming in to a circle with three lanes and just as many town names per sign per exit. Read fast or go around several times, then jump into the traffic to change lanes when the guy on your left does, close your eyes and pray.

Carrara is not that big of a town, but we seemed to have spent a fair amount of time in it trying to get out. As Nancy said when the map

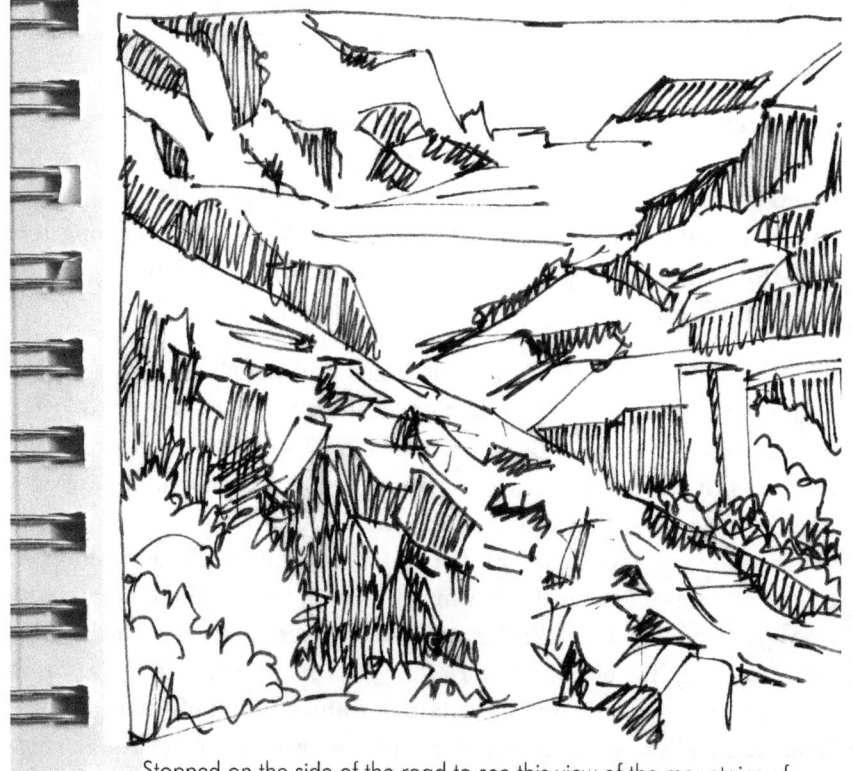

Stopped on the side of the road to see this view of the mountains of marble fields. From a distance it looks like snow on the mountains, but it is exposed marble.

failed us and we could not read the signs fast enough - head up! And so we did, the guide books we had were useless - meant for people on busses or tours - not anyone driving. Up we headed, following the road - how we got into the marble caves - to this day I do not know. The map showed one road, we found many roads with side roads, all the same width and surface. We ended up driving into the tunnels carved out of solid marble - following a truck with two large marble slabs on it's bed, and another large truck carrying marble on our butt ... yes, it was a Mercedes I could see the logo clearly in my back window he was that close. Had no idea how we got there or how we were going to get out, but forward we went deep into the marble caves - praying that the guy ahead knew where he was going and that the guy behind remembered our little Fiat was in front. Finally came to a little piece of daylight on our left and took it. It was a souvenir shop. How? Was this the right road? Hey what do you do in a souvenir shop? Yes, we bought some souvenirs and walked around and picked up some loose marble that had fallen off the trucks. Then we asked directions from the clerk on to get out. He told us to go over this rickety old bridge into another tunnel. Humm. We went another way, up to a place where they had 40 min tours of the marble caves, next one left in 40 min. Funny how we just seen the caves up close and personal. Came back down the road to the souvenir stand and saw a sign to Carrara, not the road the guy at the stand told us to take. Why are the signs always facing the wrong way? Wonder where that bridge actually took you. The song "Oh he never returned..." came to mind.

We followed marble trucks down and through the town of Carrara - imagine, these trucks filled with 80 tons of marble running through the narrow streets of town, the same streets used for the last 600+ years. We saw little villages tucked away in the hills, where workers have lived and used these same roads since before Michelangelo. According to the books, over 1000 caves have closed since the 1500's, and only over 100 remain, yet when we were 30 km from Carrera on the toll road we saw the mountains in the distance all white, not with snow, but with exposed marble. As our kids say, "That was awesome."

Around the town and off to the Cinque Terre. Five little towns on the coast built into the cliffs, settled by anchovy fishermen, wine and olive farmers. The towns are connected by a train and a walkway for hiking. No cars except locals are allowed in.

Our plan had always been to go to the farthest town south, Riomaggiore and walk the trail to the next town Manarola, about a 20 min. walk, then back again. No way we could walk the entire trail, taking many hours, and we were not really interested in taking the train to quickly

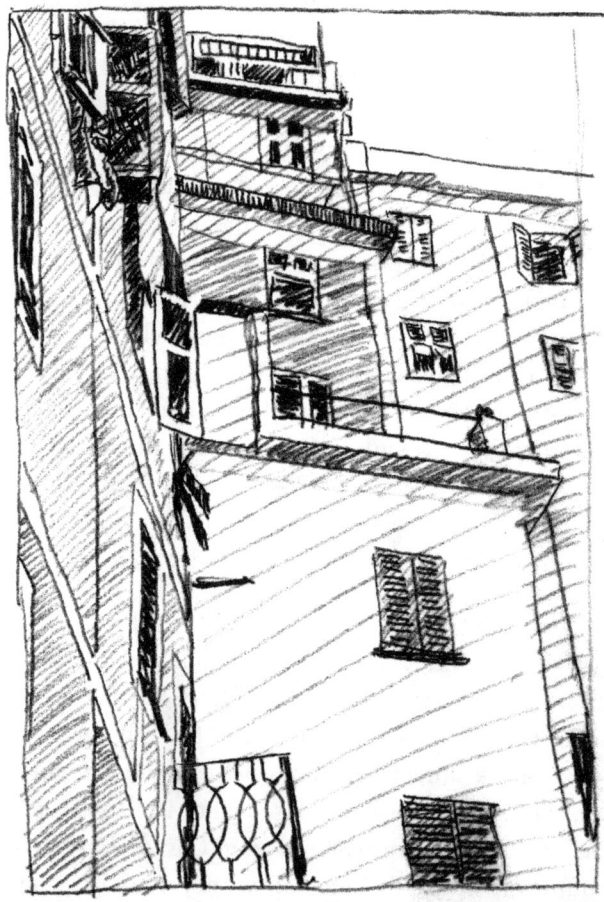

Great painting of the colorful buildings of the Cinque Terre. A more detailed drawing for the painting - this is in the town of Riomaggiorie. Love the colors but also drawn to the shapes and angles. Love the texture - the window blinds against the stone walls.

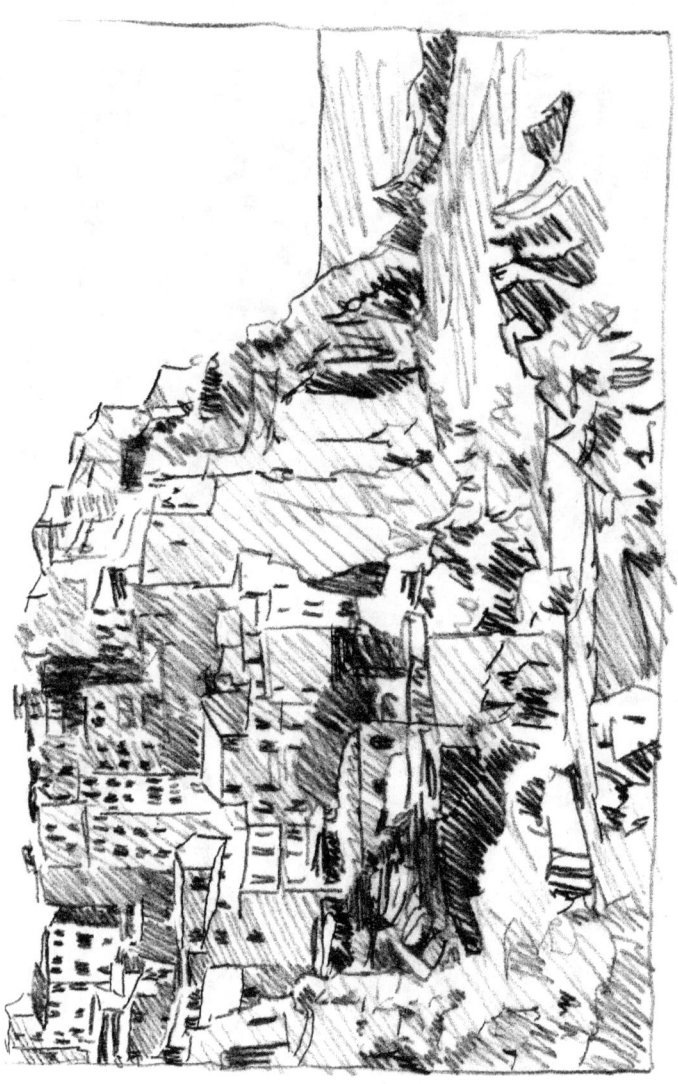

This needs to be a large painting to get in all of the buildings and colors. Manarola, a small town built into the cliffs. Emerald green of the Mediterranean Sea and the purple storm clouds coming in over the water emphasize the brilliant colors and shadows. When I paint this, I want the boats in the foreground to be the center of interest and lead your eye into the painting. So I will put them in intense sunlight and gray back the colors a bit in the town and sky. This is a complex painting so this is one of many pencil drawings to get the values correct. I will spend many days doing the final drawing on the canvas.

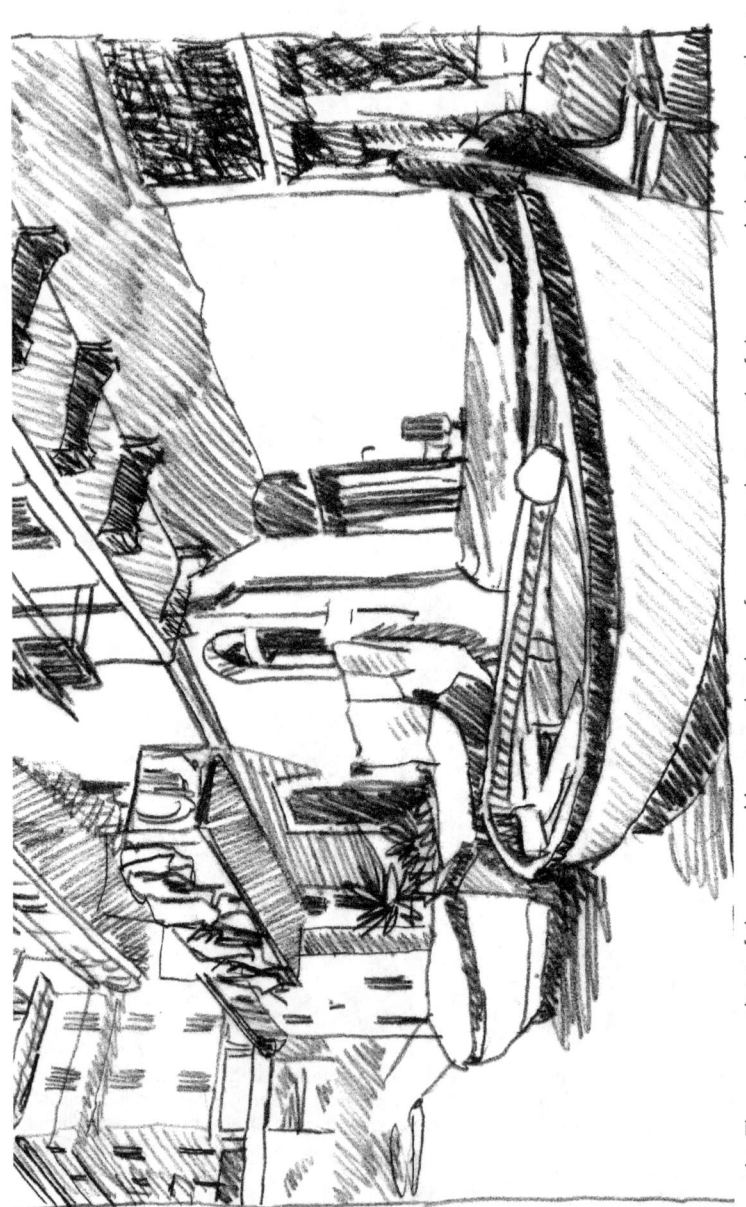

Manarola. They are anchovie fishermen and because they have few cars in the town the fishermen park their boats on the street infront of their house. The boats are on rollers so the men just push the boats to the ramps and down into the water. Beautiful colors and the front boat is white with a great teak trim. The storm was coming in so many of the boats had covers over them. This is a more detailed pencil sketch to get the values right. This piece will also became a powerful vertical painting.

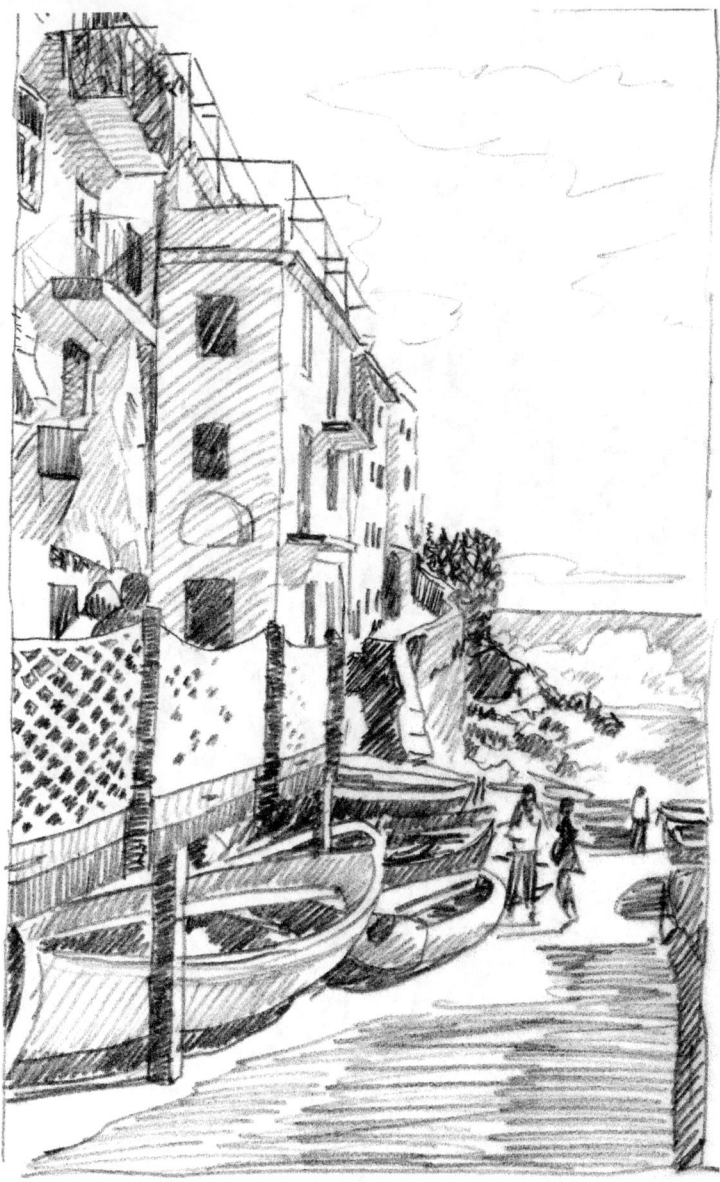

Pencil sketch for painting. Typical scene in Riomaggiorie, here the boats are stored under a little restaurant tucked away on one of the little side streets. This is one of the ramps used to launch the boats, a set up of people if I ever saw one. In the background at the waters edge is a single woman (Nancy), closer in is a family - a couple and the woman is pregnant. In the foreground at the restaurant is an older couple enjoying the day and each others company. The Cycle of Life.

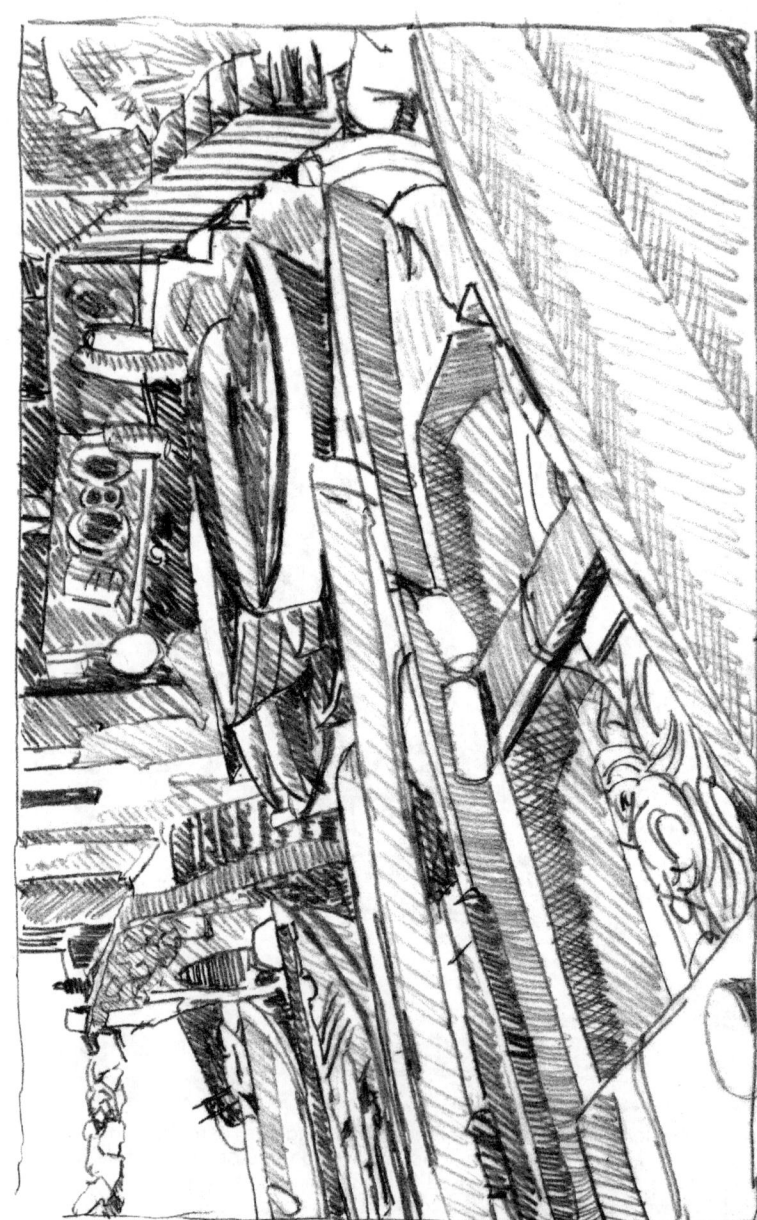

Detailed pencil sketch for painting. Riomaggiorie again. Great painting of not only the brilliant colors of the boats, red, yellow, orange, and blue, but also the pattern. The boats are stacked in one of the ramp areas- they are packed like sardines and the colors are so intense they look fake.

see the other towns. We wanted to spend some time in just a couple of towns as we do not have the energy to hike that much.

We went through the harbor town of La Spezia, finally got through town, busy little town with a lot of traffic and hills - beautiful drive with views of the sea. With the black BMW on my butt and 25 feet notice before a hard right turn, we missed the turn off for Riomaggiore, so we went to Manarola instead. Found a parking lot that was manned, parked and started walking the terraced hills down to the sea and the town. A fun little place for photos and sketches. The colors are amazing ... the buildings are painted pinks, pumpkin, terra cotta, pale blues, yellows, whites and red. Nancy and I had lunch in a little place off the main street, This town is known for it's fresh anchovies, olives, and white wine. So we tried them all. Not keen on white wine, but it was a good semi-dry slightly fruity, the anchovies were not what we are use to in the cans. They were whole silver skinned fish on bread smothered in local olive oil, very yummy, and a small plate of local salumies and a jar of olives. Really nice and refreshing after our walk. All the time we were there, there were storm clouds and thunder, we were use to that living on the coast ourselves. We bought our tickets for the hike to the next town (a one day pass as it's a National Park). and walked to Riomaggiore the first town, a 20 min walk ... on the Via dell'Amore, the lover's walk.

All along the path people put up locks ... to their hearts. Photo ops throughout, us included. We took pixs of couples and they took our photo snuggling in one of the special chairs on the trail and kissing. Hey in Italy ...

In the town of Riomaggiore we had some more gelato - the lemon was great, light and pucker up tart. Because of the storm, the beach was closed - red flags - so we wanderered around town. Completely worn out just hiking those first two towns, up and down and all around, some steep hills. The 90 min. hike to the next town was closed and you could only get there by train. Our stamina was wearing out so we slowly walked to the car, all up hill and back to our little B&B.

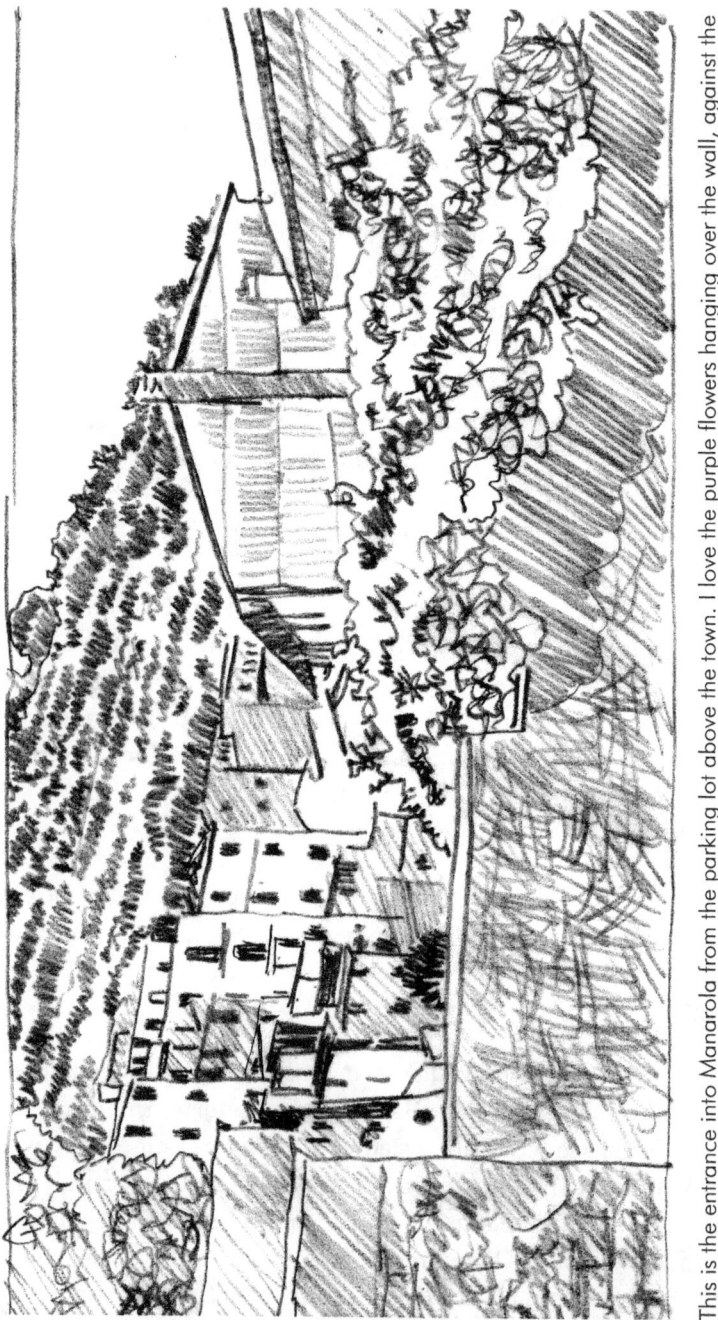

This is the entrance into Manarola from the parking lot above the town. I love the purple flowers hanging over the wall, against the dark gray wall the colors are intense. In this painting I will show the terraces of the vineyards in the background that surround the town. The hectic colors and patterns of the town in the midground and the peace and tranquility of the foreground with only the purple flowers and green leaves. This is a pencil sketch for the final painting.

*This has run a bit long so I will spare you our trip back except to say that sitting in the road of La Rocca was a couple ahead of us who decided to explain to each other why they should not be a couple anymore. She got into the car that was parked in the middle of the road and took off. He went back into the building with some interesting gestures and comments on life.

Our cuisine tonight was 3 sandwiches and an unknown pastry from a deli that was closing, and a bottle of well deserved wine we had in our room.

SAN GERVASIO - LUCCA

Day 6 - Sept. 20

As I write this days events at 5:30 pm sitting on our little terrace outside our room, I am reminded of a bit of wisdom I have heard over the years ... "Patience Grasshopper". Another gulp of wine. I did not have an ulcer before today, but there are no guarantees now.

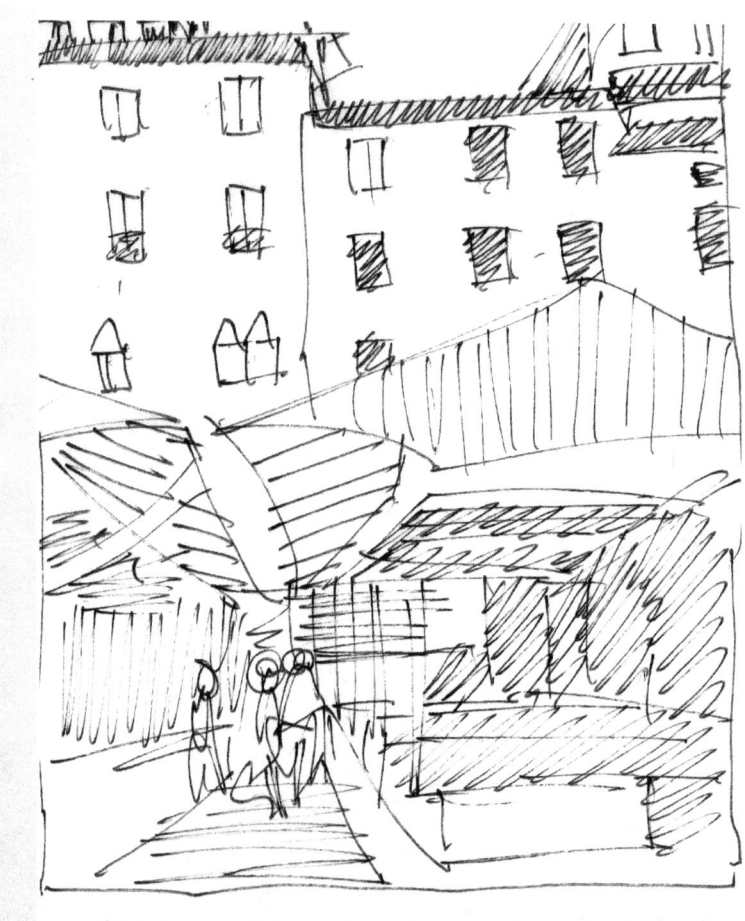

Lucca - this is the marketplace in the main square. It was after 1:30 in the afternoon and all of the retail stores were closed until 3:30. In the outdoor market, the front stalls here are closed, but there is still activity in the rest of the area. Again, the brilliant colors and patterns of the awnings against the muted town colors.

The day started out exceedingly well, blue sky with puffy white clouds, breakfast on the large patio and Wi-Fi that worked enough to download 63 email messages. One was from the Cortile gallery in Massachusetts, where I just placed two sculptures and three paintings in a show, saying they sold another bronze of "The Poet". That makes two sculptures and one painting since the show opened Labor Day weekend - almost 3 weeks - so I emailed them and our kids. Oooops, dropped signal, no emails or calls out.

With high spirits, our road map and the Rick Steves' map of Lucca, we head out - about 40 mins. away. As bad as the road signs have been, signs to Lucca are almost non existent. When we finally got there, well, fortunately it is a circular walled city. With our trusty Steves' book, complete with map we had every intention of doing Lucca his way. Do NOT drive inside the city walls, park at one of the many parking lots or ticketed spaces, notice those marked on my map- beware of parking in the wrong area. Sound advice, but not in the real world of multiple round abouts with four lanes of converging traffic.

The people in Washington D.C. talk about the horrors of Dupont Circle where you may end up going around it for days. They have not been in Lucca. I can't describe it except to say - go to Pisa and walk to Lucca - it will take you longer, but it will be healthier. NO street signs visible to drivers, small parking signs that you see between cars going every which way. We found ourselves inside the walled city driving behind a local city bus, we passed ticketed parking spaces on the side of the road for €1/hr, and an underground parking lot. But no, Steves says don't do it, so we went back out of the city walls into the mayhem. When your navigator says not too kindly that she does not know where we are - it's not on the map, you are in some serious doodoo.

Now as you read these journal entries you may think we are incompetent boobs when it comes to driving. Well, let me tell you - we were at the B&B with three other couples. They were all from Germany, all use to driving in European countries besides Germany and they all had horror stories similar to ours when it came to the roads in Italy. One couple walked all around the wall of Lucca trying to find the street they parked their car on - 3 hours they walked. Another couple took twice as long to get back from Siena as it should have - round about nightmares and lack of signage. So, maybe it is not just us.

I don't know how, but we got back into the city wall, pulled into the underground parking garage for €2/hr, and we were still alive and talking to each other. We threw away the Rick Steves' book with the Lucca map - worse than useless.

Nancy and I walked around town following the few tourists there were, but we got there after 1pm. In Italy most stores shut down from 1-3:30pm daily. That left us with restaurants and the outdoor market. After an hour, we were exhausted , emotionally more than anything else. Wandered the streets but were burned out. We walked the walls in the sun and peace and took pics and just enjoyed the town from it's walls. The locals we have met in our travels 99% of the time were very nice people, even when we did not talk the same language. And they turned out to be very helpful to us tourists.

It was a piece of cake getting out of Lucca and back to the safety of the backroads which we now knew how to navigate. Tired, hungry worn out, we traveled to a little town near our B&B, I forget which, to get something to eat ... a grocery store - so we picked up some wonderful cheeses we could not pronounce, several meats and salami, fresh baked bread. We ate our lunch on our patio with a bottle of local wine and Nancy went for a swim as I am writing this.

We are waiting for 7:30 to come when our host Daniele will prepare a Tuscan feast. The wine cellar tables are set for 13 people and the smells are intoxicating already. Daniele is a quiet man, speaks only Italian, and is a hard working man who keeps the farm running smoothly so Caroline can take care of us. More tomorrow as tonight will be late.

Day 7 - Sept. 21

The dinner last night was marvelous. Eleven people plus Nancy and me.

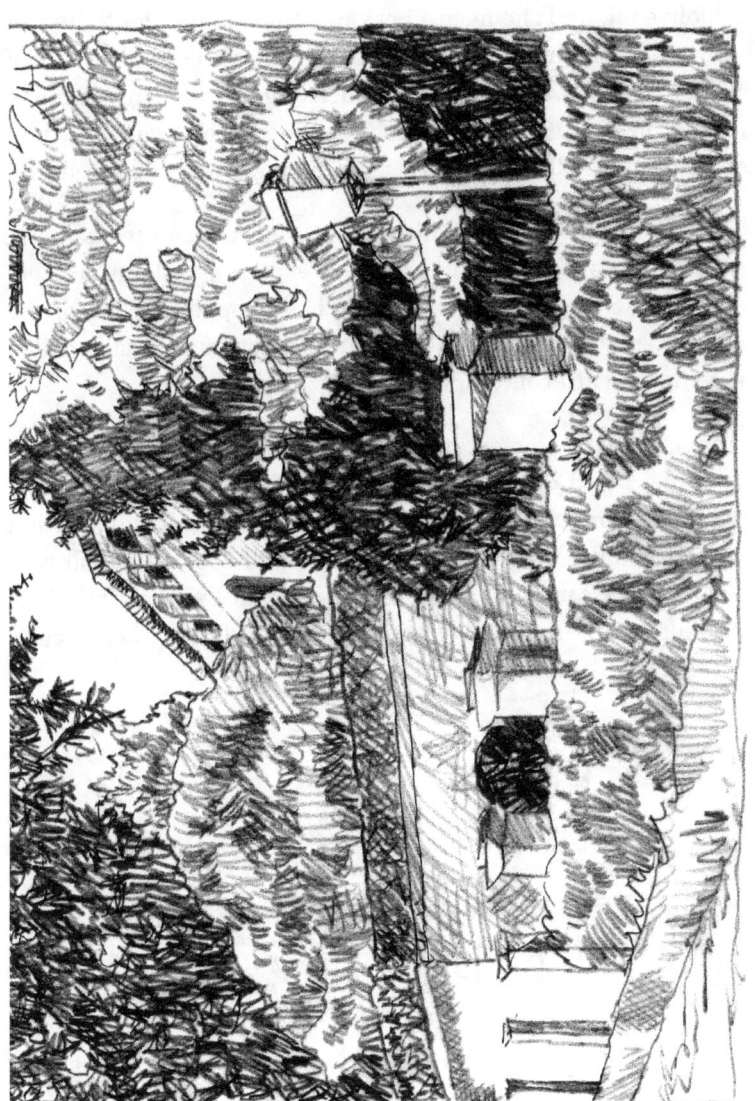

The main street of San Gervasio. This should be a nice little painting, architecture and nature in balance forming this quaint painting. The colors and textures of the walls of stone going in different directions intertwined with the controlled foliage. In the afternoon sun this whole scene has turned into a yellow-green image as the colors have warmed up the cool stone. Detail pencil sketch for final painting.

We started out with 3 types of brochette - basil, a mushroom in sauce, and a meat ragu. Followed by a pasta dish of bacon in a spicy ragu sauce. The main coarse was oven roasted potatoes in thyme, white beans with olive oil, and the meat - pork roast marinated for 2 days in a thyme, olive oil, pine nut and basil mixture then covered in a crust of salt, roasted and sliced. For dessert the chef's signature dish, tiramisu. Plus the wines flowed, prosecco (italian sparkling wine), local white and red wines, and limoncello. Don't forget the espresso and cappuccinos.

Daniele, Caroline's husband who also ran the farm, was the chef, and he does this dinner once a week if there are enough people interested. Two couples from Switzerland, not staying here stopped in just for the dinner. Dinner started precisely at 7:30 and Nancy and I finally called it a night sometime after midnight.

As you can imagine the conversations were all over the board. The others at our table; Petra & Frank, Sandra & Guido (with a young lady who works for Sandra who's name I have forgotten, sorry) and Martina & Manfred, although all from Germany they also spoke English well enough for us to all communicate. Talk went from the economy, kids and grand kids (we were the oldest and with grand kids), healthcare,

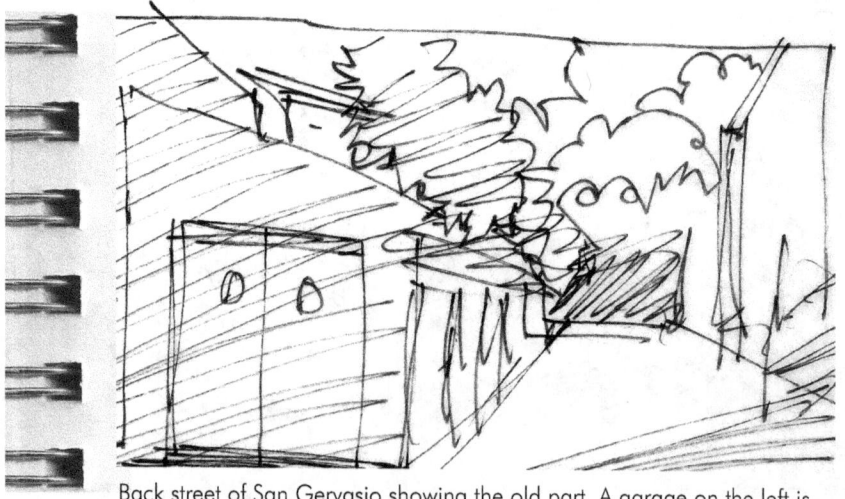

Back street of San Gervasio showing the old part. A garage on the left is falling apart. Looks to be centuries old.

politics, the Euro nation, educational systems, the whole gamut. It is interesting how others see Americans and how Americans see the rest of the world. The truths of each culture were very enlightening. When I asked if Germany was going to bail out the Greeks, they all shrugged and said Germany bails out all of Europe.

All in all a wonderful night with some extremely interesting people and new friends to stay with when we travel to Germany.

Breakfast was a little quieter than usual, then off we went for our day trip, the seaside resorts, an easy drive on the toll roads. These seaside towns, Forte dei Marmi and Pietrassanta are for the elite of Europe. The street market on Wednesday was not inexpensive knock offs, but the real deals, like the Nike outlet stores, just located in the streets. We arrived at about noon - the markets open at 8:30, and at 1pm, they started to close down and pack up the tents. All the brick and mortar stores also close including Gucci from 1-3:30. Then they open again until 8pm. It was a short relaxing day/drive for us - we drove back to the B&B had some wine, the meats and cheeses, etc. from our grocery foray the day before.

I walked to the center of San Gervasio, the 11th century hamlet we stayed in, a 3 min. walk, took photos for paintings and sketched. This hamlet and the church here are over 1000 years old, and still being used. I sit down on a little wall and sketch and just imagine all the history this church has seen and been a part of. It was locked and there was no one around, so I could not see inside. Simple construction, very durable, and still usable, I wonder how many of our buildings in the U.S. built by the first colonists will be around in 300-400 years?

When I got back to the room, Nancy had taken a swim and we sat and talked and drank some wine with our neighbors for a couple of hours before Nancy and I went to dinner. Hey, we said we were going to eat and drink our way through Tuscany so we are trying to do our best.

The restaurant is the best in the area, only open Wed - Sat. A real fun place with a wild and crazy owner (younger than us and dressed to the nines in heels and a lot of jewelry). Like her staff - she is constantly running form table to table as any good host does and was talking faster than Nancy - in Italian, English and German. It was a long drive from our room, 4 min. by narrow back roads, and no, we did not get lost - hey only one road, easy.

In the kitchen was Mama - short, stocky, in a nice black dress, pearl necklace and earrings, she ran the kitchen of 2 other cooks. Know where the daughter got her style from. The food - a section of the restaurant had two tables about 12' long each was covered in Antipasti - help yourself -every kind of thing you can imagine. From pear slices with cheese, to liver pate, every kind of salumi to pickled octopus (Nancy tried and like that one). Then we each had a pasta dish - gnocchi and rigatoni - then the owner made us a dessert plate from the tables out front. No menus - you order what they are making that day - but we did not have room for a main coarse. The wine was very local - their wine, the grapes were from their vineyard across the road. The local food and wines in Tuscany are so rich and flavorful, like the soil around them. An excellent dinner with some really fun people. The music was Madonna, Springstein, Clapton, BB King. The owner was singing along when no one was looking. Home and to bed. Tomorrow Firenze.

Drawing on the right is a market street in Firenze. Lots of people looking in a lot of small store fronts. Again the red awnings and the multicolors of the clothes of the people in the street. I am struck by the colors and textures against the sedate colors of the buildings in the background. As a painting it might be too busy, but it was stunning to see.

FIRENZE

Day 8 - Sept. 22

Last morning in the beautiful hills of Tuscany. After breakfast we said goodbye to all our new friends - and hit the road. Everyone said do not drive in Firenze - take the train. After our experience in Lucca we were only too happy to. So we drove to the Pisa airport and dropped off the rental car. A piece of cake. From the airport we got the train €1.20 to the Pisa train station, then into the station and got two tickets to Firenze - €5.90 ea. Easily to the right platform, on to the train and a one hour ride in an air conditioned car. Got to our destination, walked out of the train station and in five minutes we were in our hotel. Not the same experience we had in Rome and their train station. Pisa and Firenze were well marked stations, clean and fast and a pleasure to travel.

Dean, our local wine merchant suggested a little hotel he stayed in when in Italy, only a block from the Duomo, the Hotel Centrale. The hotel had just finished some renovations and they put us in one of the new rooms. Very classy a nice way to end our trip. The people were very nice & helpful. Thanks Dean.

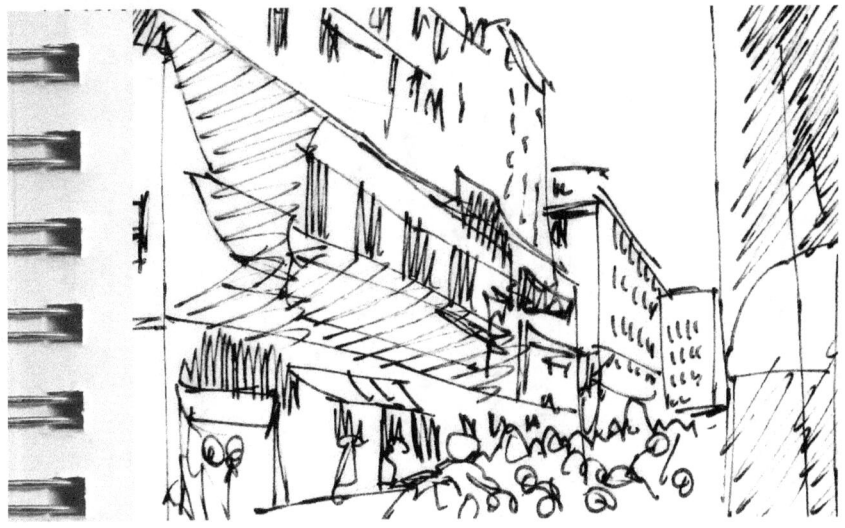

We walked to the closest little square and had lunch outside at one of the many little restaurants. Shopped in the outdoor market at the leather stalls. Nancy bought and I schlepped. Back to the hotel for a rest until dinner @ 7:30ish. Before dinner we walked around the Duomo a whole different look to the place at dusk. Found a little place to eat - spaghetti carbonara and mussels in a marinara sauce - some local wine. We ate outside and paid the cover charge - but the night was too beautiful to be inside and it was real warm. Funny how all of the places to eat here charged a cover to sit inside or outside, but not if you stand at the counter - but most did not have counters. Just another way to get a bit more, cover charges we encountered were from €.50 ea to €2.50 ea. and the size of the establishment had nothing to do with the price.

After dinner, we walked around some more and I smoked a cigar - had another galato, raspberry and a mocha this time. Very good, but the lemon is still the best. How good of an evening is this? Walking in Firenze around the Duomo with my love - listening to a woman in front of the Duomo singing Ava Marie, eating galato and smoking a cigar. I could get use to this.

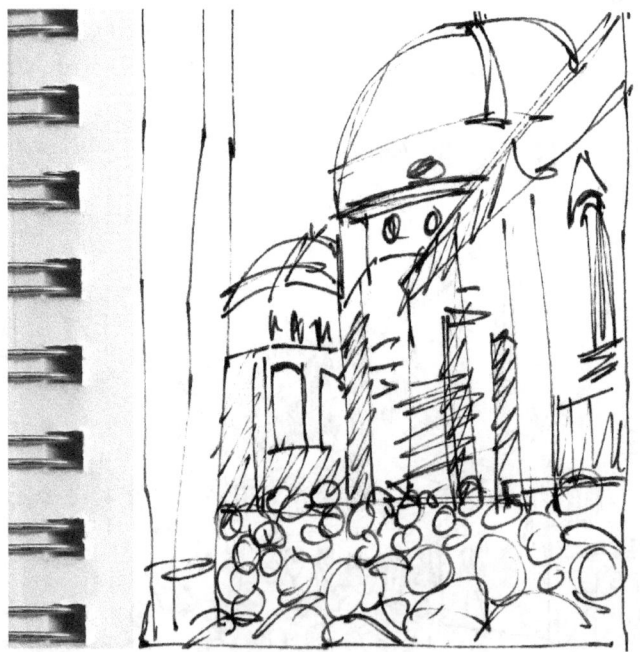

As we stepped out of our hotel in Firenze and turned left there was the town square. That close to the action but we did not hear the noise as our room was in the back of the hotel.

The drawing on the right page is of one of the Prisoners by Michelangelo.

Day 9 - Sept. 23

We woke up at 8:15 - showered and walked up to breakfast on the second floor - typical fruits, coffee, cheese, ham, breads, cold cereals and croissants - but a treat today - a hard boiled egg. Died and went to heaven. Then off to see the "David" at the Galleria dell'Accademie. We have reservations for 10:15, our hotel made the reservations for us for this and the Uffizi Gallery tomorrow. Two blocks to the Duomo then four more to the gallery.

Had to put our stuff and us through the metal detector, then pay the fee, cash only and exact change - in all the things we read, including their web site, there was no mention of this. Also, it was not €9.50 each but €15 ea. they had a "special exhibit" and charged more. Fortunately we had the exact cash. The reserved line we were in was longer than the other line, but they had to wait as we went in first.

The Accademie that houses the "David" also has the "Prisoners" - and

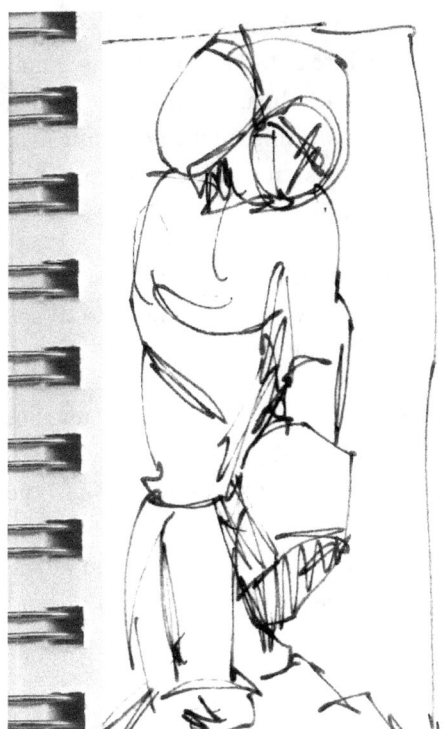

can be seen in 1/2 hour. Photos are not allowed, and the guards had to keep telling people. I doubt that camera flashes can harm 600 year old carved marble, but them's the rules. They herd you into some minor side rooms with the "special exhibit" then into the hall with the David under a dome. Again, the rooms are small compared to the photos I have seen.

Nancy and I spent most of our time walking down the hallway and stopping at each "Prisoner" - unfinished carved from a beautiful yellowish marble - from the Carrera marble fields we were in earlier in the trip. I could get up close, inches away, unrestricted and see all the tool marks and tell exactly which chisel Michelangelo used to cut and shape the marble. These unfinished pieces and the two Slaves in Paris are my favorite pieces by him. You can see and feel the power and energy and massive shapes as they are emerging out of the marble slab. The shapes of the limbs are so bulky and chunky, legs like massive tree trunks before he refined and polished his work. It looks like he has cut the shape sizes in half as he refined them and molded the muscles.

The exhibit is very well done as you walk by these large unfinished pieces and at the end of the hallway is the "David". Everything written about this piece is true - and it is best to be seen close up and from below, then the proportions are correct. What impresses me is the power of the piece at a distance, and up close the muscles, and curves and counter curves the contrapasto and the way the skin becomes transparent you can see the veins of the body under the surface of the marble - white marble. And to think this block of marble was rejected by all the artists as being flawed - one of the reasons Michelangelo was given the marble. *Note, in my diary I go into detail as to how the scholars say Michelangelo carved his marble, and I heard many tour guides expound on that as well, but I will spare you this, just know that as a sculptor of marble, the experts are wrong. Ask me sometime when you have a lot of time and I will explain it to you.

I spent many hours looking at the "Prisoners" and the "David" and Nancy sat and was patient with me. I have waited a long time to see these pieces, so I was not to be hurried. Thanks Nancy.

Then we walked through the markets again - the open street market then found the building that housed the food stalls. Inside there were foods of all kind, and wines and butchers with all kinds of meats, some unrecognizable - and tables to sit to eat. Found a couple of interesting places, but walked around to see it all before deciding. We stood at the counter and ordered a pinini and a feta cheese and tomato salad and gnocchi and they showed us to a table. Good hearty cheap food along with the sights and smells of the market.

After eating we wandered around the streets awhile -then to the Medici Chapel that had the tomb of the Medici's with sculptures by Michelangelo - Dawn, Dusk, Day & Night plus the Medici kids. We missed the chapel several times because we were looking for signs, and a big building. It is a small building and the sign is by the door on the building, 8"

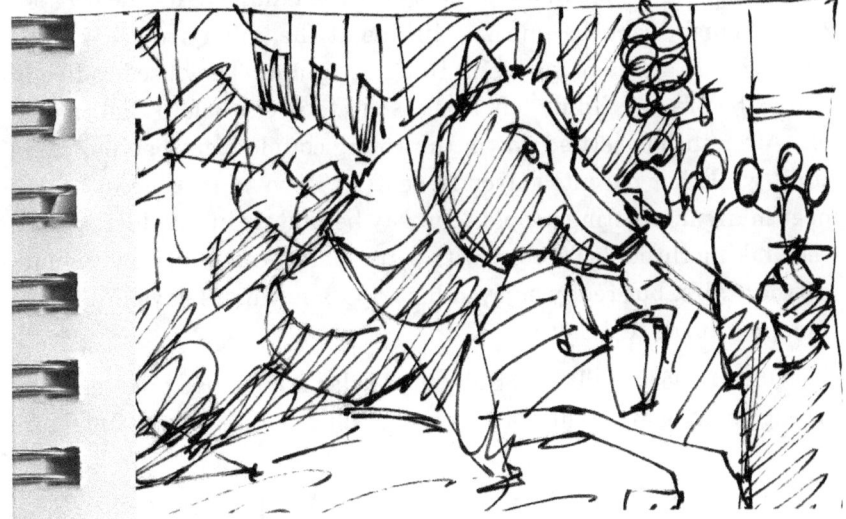

A bronze statue of a wild boar outside of the covered market. People would rub his snout for good luck.

x 12" carved in the stone. Disney needs to come to Italy and show them how to get people to a place and moved through orderly lines.

We walked right into the chapel, paid our €6 ea. went through the metal detectors and bingo - a quick tour through the first floor (it was being restored), up the narrow winding staircase, marble, to the small room where the tomb is. This entire room was designed, and carved, tombs and sculpture by Michelangelo. When Michelangelo was young he lived with the Medici's and knew and loved them, so for him, this was a labor of love and honor to his friends.

Again a lot to see, and took the time, oh, again no cameras.

Back to the hotel and off to dinner around 8. Same old thing, good dinner, crazy waiter, smoked a cigar and ate gelato and walked with Nancy arm in arm around the Duomo.

michael tieman

Day 10 - Sept. 24

Up at 8:15 again - beautiful morning - sun all day supposed to be a high
of 85. Had breakfast at the hotel and off we went to the Uffizi. Nice 10
min. walk - followed the crowds, finally a small directional sign. Being
Saturday more people in the streets - a lot of families. Also heard a lot
more English from the tourists. In line at the gallery to get in - the
young couple ahead of us live in Hong Kong now. They used to live in
Seattle before her family left Hong Kong the year before the English
left. After things settled down, the young couple went back to Hong
Kong, while her parents stayed in Seattle. Traveling is a great way to
meet many interesting people. The guy behind us in line just spent a
week biking through Tuscany with a group. He was sore, slowly climb-
ing the stairs, but really enjoyed his trip - a few more days in Firenze
then he returns to Atlanta.

The Uffizi gallery, built in 1581 by the Medici family, had an interesting
arrangement of art - sculpture along the walls - arranged as a full figure

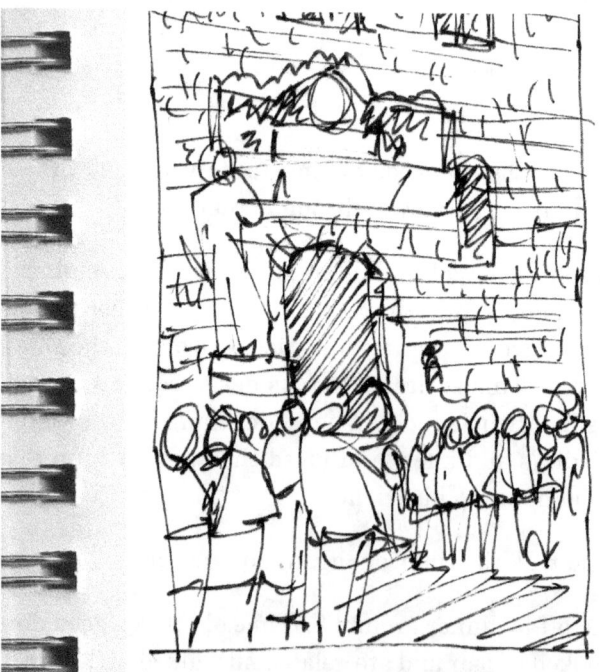

The original outdoor
setting where David
stood before someone
attacked him and it
was sent to it's present
indoor location. The
ever present crowd of
Asians taking a gazillion
photos.

A great painting, so I have made a more detailed pencil drawing that I will use as a guide for values and structure on the final painting. This is the backside of the Ponte Vecchio bridge of gold. The paint is peeling off, shutters arer broken and coming down. What fantastic colors and textures and the play of light and shadows.

followed by 2 busts - all throughout the gallery halls. Again no cameras allowed. Above the sculptures in the main halls were paintings all the same size of the important people of the time. The side rooms held tapestries and paintings. We went into the Raphael, DiVinci, Michelangelo, Durer, and Rembrant rooms - it was strange that the rooms contained pieces from many other artists and just one or two from the main artist. Saw the Birth of Venus painting - large and beautiful and beside it was a plaster relief of the painting so blind people could feel the painting. The original braille painting. The Rembrant room was probably the most disappointing, only three small paintings of his - and the Durer room had a few paintings, but none of his drawings which he was famous for.

All in all it was impressive. However, the sculptures were copies of the Roman pieces that they had copied from the Greeks. Yet, thay are 700 years old plus. Before the Impressionistic period, which began in the mid 1800's, an artist was usually supported by a wealthy patron or won commissions from cities or the church. There were no art galleries as we see them today. An artist had to be extremely talented and well connected, or worked as a peon in a studio.

From here to the Ponte Vecchio bridge- the oldest of Firenzie's six bridges built around 1340's and in the 15th century it became the bridge of Gold - Nancy was in heaven.

All the gold, silver and gemstones you can imagine. Nancy wanted to buy several rings all the same style for friends at one of the stores. They did not have enough, so one of the clerks went to their other ten stores on the bridge to find the rest of the rings. And she did. You cannot believe the wealth on that bridge, yet it is old and delapadated with the smelly Arno river running under the bridge.

Lunch - pizza and wine and more outdoor markets then to the Palazzo Vecchio, the town hall of Firenzie started in 1299, where the "David" originally stood for some 300 years. A copy is there now. In an outdoor sculpture garden is housed the sculpture, "The Rape of the Sabine Woman".

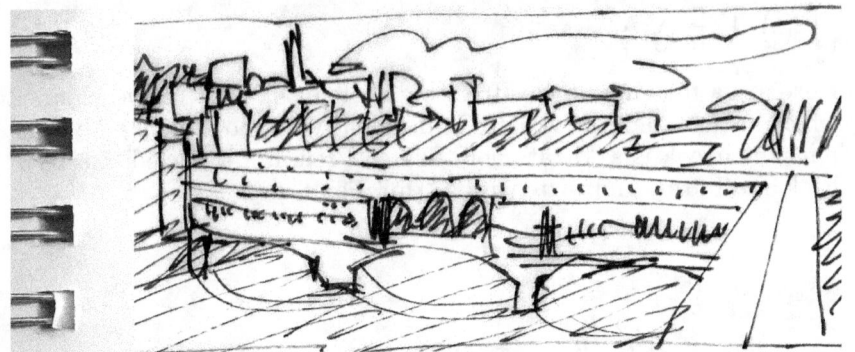

Ponte Vecchio bridge looking out of the windows from the Uffizi Gallery

Back to the hotel to relax before dinner and our last night in Italy - tomorrow we fly to Munich, Chicago and finally ending in Portland at 11:30 pm. We will pick up our car at the airport and drive home to Cannon Beach to sleep in our own bed.

This is my last entry. Italy was a wonderful experience, and yes, we ate and drank our way through Tuscany but we also got some culture.

Ciao

NOTES:

Here are a few more pages from my sketchbook that I have scanned which include some of the notes I take along with the sketches. My journal/sketchbook is a "Strathmore Sketch Premium Recycled" 5.5"x8.5" book and I draw and write with a "DuraPoint" pen.

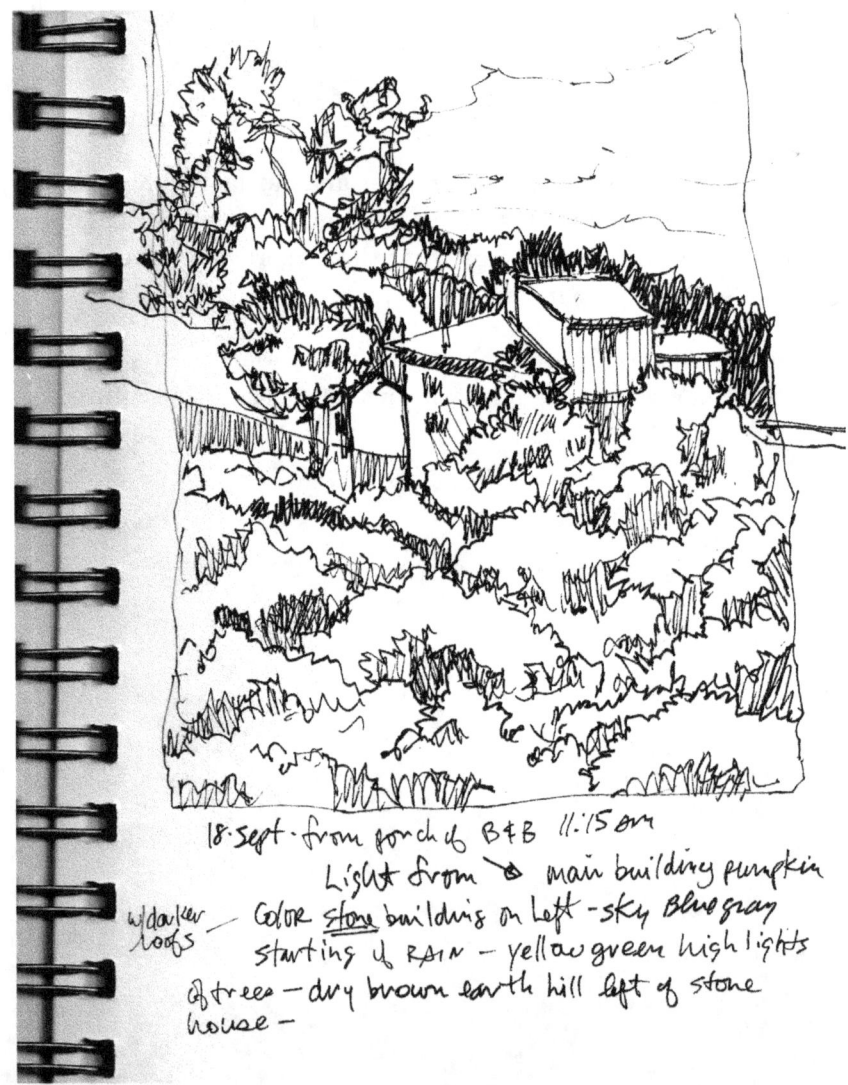

18·Sept·from porch of B&B 11:15 am
Light from → main building pumpkin
w/darker — Color stone buildings on left -sky Blue gray
roofs   starting to RAIN — yellow green high lights
of trees — dry brown earth hill left of stone
house —

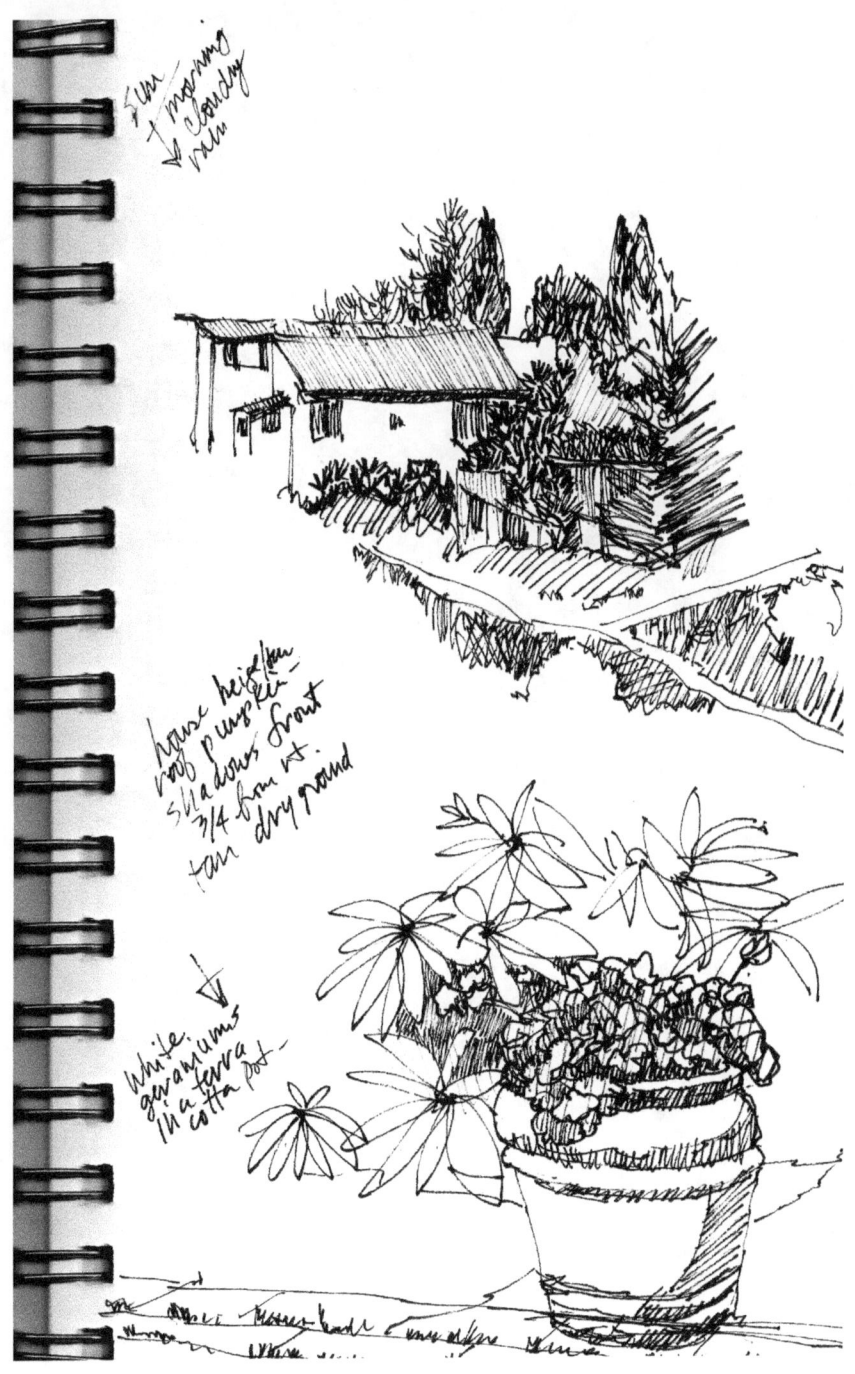

www.ingramcontent.com/pod-product-compliance
Lightning Source LLC
Chambersburg PA
CBHW072259170526
45158CB00003BA/1108